IMAGES
of America

PORTER

D1202497

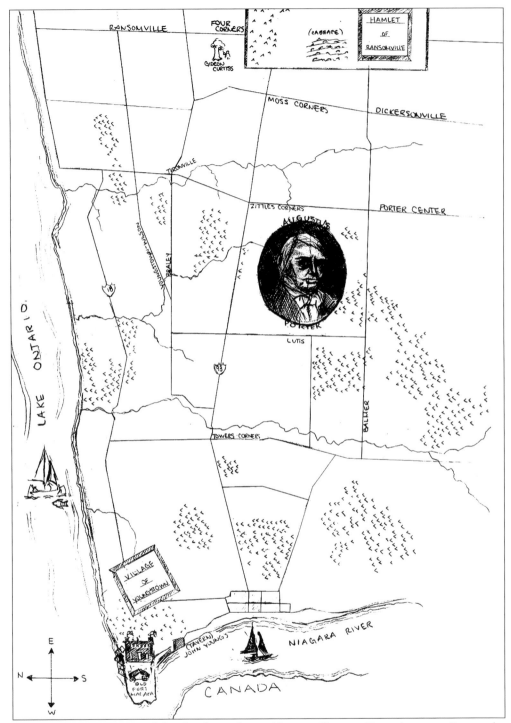

TOWN OF PORTER. Named for the first judge in Niagara County, Hon. Augustus Porter, the town of Porter was formed on June 1, 1812, by an act of the New York State legislature. The first recorded town meeting was held on April 11, 1815. This map was drawn by Stephanie Lester, an art major and resident of Porter. (Courtesy of Stephanie Lester.)

IMAGES
of America

PORTER

Suzanne Simon Dietz

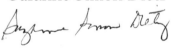

ARCADIA

Published by Arcadia Publishing
Charleston SC, Chicago IL, Portsmouth NH, San Francisco CA

Printed in Great Britain

Library of Congress Catalog Card Number: 2005926874

For all general information contact Arcadia Publishing at:
Telephone 843-853-2070
Fax 843-853-0044
E-mail sales@arcadiapublishing.com
For customer service and orders:
Toll-Free 1-888-313-2665

Visit us on the internet at http://www.arcadiapublishing.com

AERIAL VIEW. Porter's history has been shaped by the strategic military position of Fort Niagara. This aerial photograph from the late 1950s displays much of the peaceful town's lands and the work ethic of farmers throughout almost two centuries. (Courtesy of the Old Fort Niagara Association Inc.)

CONTENTS

ACKNOWLEDGMENTS

This story began with the marriage to a Porter farm boy with deep roots in the town's dirt, my beloved husband, Raymond Dietz. His love, support, and encouragement are the spine of this text, for which I am deeply grateful. The legacies and lessons of my father, John Victor Simon, particularly his love of history, and a desire for truth fueled by my high school history teacher, Miss Grotowska, a member of the French underground and a Holocaust survivor, strengthened this journey. All in the town of Porter owe a debt to the contributions of those who worked tirelessly to preserve our history and to our ancestors who created it.

I am grateful to my sister Nannette Simon for her technical assistance and for carrying computers and scanners from one museum to another. I am also very thankful to the following people and organizations who contributed photographs and stories: Betty Allen, Mary Ellen Aureli, Priscilla Parker Baker, Margaret S. Beard, Anne Brett, Jere Brubaker, Clyde L. Burmaster, Katherine B. Collard, Kenneth G. Diez, Nan Eagan, Phyllis Edwards, Dale Ellsworth, First Presbyterian Church, Don Glynn, Lawrence W. Grimm, Cora Gushee, Gary Harris, Phyllis B. Hastings, Mildred Hillman, Vee L. Housman, Phila Ibaugh, Judith A. Jackson, Janet Jachlewski, Ed Kozey, Stephanie Lester, James R. and Patricia H. Lloyd, the Niagara Falls Public Library, Sue N. Mirabelli, Msgr. J. Thomas Moran, Jeff Morrow, the Old Fort Niagara Association, William Owler, Patricia Hutchison Phillips, the Ransomville Museum, St. Bernard's Catholic Church, St. John's Episcopal Church, St. John's Lutheran Church, Betty J. Salvatore, Peggy Shear, Harold and Neal Shippy, Marge Stratton, Audrey B. Tower, Richard and Margaret Truesdale Tower, Tom Tower, the Porter Historical Society and Museum, Sandra Sanger Tuck, Don Whittaker, Edward Wojcik, and Youngstown Cold Storage.

FOREWORD

Like many communities across the nation, the town of Porter has often confronted the challenge of preserving its identity. Within the past decade, for example, some ambitious schemes touted by potential developers ran the gamut from a high-tech automotive parts plant and a classy theme park to a Thoroughbred racetrack and a fast ferry across Lake Ontario, linking the town and Toronto, one of Canada's largest cities. None of these grandiose schemes has come to fruition, but mere mention of such large-scale commercial investments stirs understandable apprehension throughout the community.

For the record, gradual changes over the centuries have not altered, for the most part, the quality of life in the 19,870 acres that comprise the northwest sector of Niagara County. It remains a community that cherishes its heritage, its lush farmlands, its classic mix of suburban and rural settings, and its unique role in Niagara frontier history. While the stories are familiar to countless local residents, Porter has another side to its colorful past, as evidenced by this concise and informative account produced by town resident Suzanne Dietz, who is also active as a writer for the Porter Historical Society. In this latest endeavor, she has contributed a significant addition to the increasingly popular Images of America series.

Without question, she has accomplished the formidable task of gleaning an impressive array of photographs from the local historical society collection and from the numerous individuals who have shared her enthusiasm for the project.

Being privy to a treasure of local history notes within the family circle also proved beneficial. Suzanne's husband, Raymond, is a great-grandson of Johann Friedrich Diez, who once owned five farms in the township.

The writer's meticulous research and concern for accuracy brings this delightful story of Porter into even sharper perspective. Enjoy.

—Don Glynn, *Niagara Falls Gazette*

INTRODUCTION

Nestled in the northwest corner of New York State is the little known Camelot of the town of Porter, rich in pages of history. Fort Niagara's imposing structure stands as evidence of the country's conflicts. This community developed around the fort at the intersection of the Niagara River waters and the deep recesses of Lake Ontario.

On a warm summer's night in Porter, always 10 degrees cooler than its neighbor of Lewiston due to lake breezes, people gather in Falkner Park for summer concerts. Echoes of Doc Falkner, who arrived in 1875 and, with his son, served the community as doctor for almost 100 years, resound. Musket fire from the fort and the hourly pealing bells of St. Bernard's Church can be heard. Fishermen return from a day on the waters with their trailers and boats. On the sidewalks, children and adults savor ice-cream cones from the Gas and Grille or the Village Ice Cream Shop. It is Friday night in Youngstown, and Mayor Neil Riordan greets the townspeople: "Welcome to Mayberry." It seems that this is so, as children swing and slide and parents and grandparents sit on lawn chairs or blankets, enjoying the sounds of jazz, barbershop quartets, and bagpipers.

As we journey through time, the breezes of the past swirl up from Water Street amidst the rainbow of sailboats moored in front of the yacht club. The steamboats *Chicora* and *Cayuga* create an immense wake as they run up and down the river. The townspeople begin to leave the concert and come to the main crossroads of the Ontario House. For more than 100 years, patrons sipped a cool one on the porch here. A short distance south, near the dip in the road known as "Bloody Run," the memories of anguished cries of the bloodiest and most decisive battle of the French and Indian War disturb the peace of the moment. On July 25, 1759, the French surrendered, and the fort passed into British hands after the Battle of La Belle Famille.

Youngstown, named for Canadian John Young, fades as darkness blankets the village. The townspeople head east toward the hamlet of Ransomville on Route 93, also known as Youngstown-Lockport Road, the window to the farms. Apple trees and peach trees line the road as an honor guard. The winter wheat has awoken from its dormancy, and the stalks that in late August will be baled for straw stand at attention. Orchard sprayers whine in the background of the night sounds. During a dry spell, the vibration of the water pumping on cabbage and corn fields helps wet the summer dust and lowers the water pressure throughout the town. The farm names of pioneers and early settlers roll by through their descendants' farms and stand as a tribute to those whose workday knows no limits. The age of tractors and orchard sprayers vanishes as the past becomes clearer. Farmers with sweat dripping from their brows behind their precious team of horses are shouting "gee" and "haw" as they turn at the end of a row.

The main road's intersections have borne the names of the farmers: Tower, Zittle, Hand, Moss, and Quade Corners. Sheltered amidst the farm community, the bells on the rural schools scattered across the town are silent now. The faint echo of young scholars learning to read and write at Tower's Corners and Porter-Center can be heard. In the winter, the teacher arrived early to start the fire with hope the inkwells would thaw before the end of the day.

The hustle and bustle from the Ransomville Fire Company, the gathering center for the hamlet, is a short ride across town. Celebrations, fund-raisers for those less fortunate, and the annual Cabbage Festival demonstrate the neighborly spirit of the community. The sharp crackling of the timbers from the heart of the hamlet by Gideon Curtiss's ax vibrates the early frontier. The community was carved by his purchase of property from the Holland Land Company in 1817. The passionate community spirit and enterprise that followed are like the waves from the strong winds across Lake Ontario. From the timbers Curtiss felled came the log cabin that served as a tavern on the east side of town.

The sawmill east of Quade's Corners, later known as Four Corners, the main intersection in Ransomville, cuts the boards for the homes and buildings that follow. Farmers come for barrels at the cooperage and baskets from the basket factory. The mounds of apples waiting for processing at Swigert's evaporator look like rolling hills. Farmers arrive in Ransomville, named for Jehial Ransom, and gather at the Grange Hall. Ransom's Store provides supplies for decades, then gives way to today's Porter Country Mart. Farmers and townspeople talk at the big table at Johnston's Restaurant, famous since Prohibition, to discuss the news, repeat the tales of the past, and create new ones for the future.

Centuries have come and gone since the Neuter, also known as Neutral Indians, lived in the forested regions of Porter and western New York. Arrowheads and crude utensils remain as a testament to the beginnings of civilization in this hallowed town, which has made its mark in history by people passionate about their freedoms and the right to turn over the soil for their families!

One

SAILS, SALMON, AND SHIPS

VILLAGE OF YOUNGSTOWN. On October 4, 1854, the village held its first election, beginning its evolution from a small settlement and store run by businessman John Young, its namesake. (Courtesy of the Porter Museum.)

SHIPBUILDING. The *Edna K* was built in 1901 in Youngstown. George King, seen standing on the deck, told the historical society in years past, "We cut the logs in the woods on Peter Tower's Farm. . . . The logs were cut at Hosmer's Mill . . . then we sent to Lockport for a caulker." (Courtesy of the Porter Museum.)

A WALK IN THE PARK. This early-1900s view, taken from the Haskell homestead looking west, has been repeated throughout time. While taking a stroll along the river, people still enjoy the sights of our Canadian neighbor. (Courtesy of the Porter Museum.)

SS ROCHESTER. Docked at Youngstown Harbor, the *Rochester* served the Youngstown-Charlotte-Prescott route from the turn of the century to about 1915. The Eldorado Hotel, gristmill, and Haskell building are visible above the ship. (Courtesy of the Porter Museum.)

VIEW FROM THE FORT. Youngstown was an important shipping port in the 1800s. The steamer *Cayuga*, running from 1907 to 1952, is seen here, along with the Daupin Battery at the fort in the foreground of this postcard. Bob Lloyd, a descendant of the first settler of the town, tells of attending the Youngstown High School senior prom on this boat. (Courtesy of the Porter Museum.)

FORT NIAGARA BEACH. The railroad ties have been replaced by picnic tables and swimming pools. From this spot, community members continue to enjoy the sight of the deep Lake Ontario and the sailboats and fishing vessels plying its waters. (Courtesy of the Porter Museum.)

THE WATERFRONT. James Marshall, the McGowan Brothers, and others ran ferries to Niagara-on-the-Lake, Ontario. George King and his father bought out the McGowans and operated a ferry from 1917 to about 1923. Casey Fitzpatrick used to take customers across the river in a rowboat! (Courtesy of the Porter Museum.)

YOUNGSTOWN YACHT CLUB. The yacht club was organized on April 29, 1931, at a meeting at the Youngstown Fire Hall. The trustees then negotiated a lease for the Haskell property. To join, one paid $15 in initiation fees and $10 in annual dues. Some of the boards from John Young's store were used to build the present club. (Courtesy of the Porter Museum.)

THE ONEN. Denis Onen lived at 125 Lockport Street and, with his brother, had a boatbuilding business. They used the *Anna F. Onen* as a ferry between Niagara-on-the-Lake and the village in the early 1900s. Onen was also known as "Owen." (Courtesy of the Porter Museum.)

COMMERCIAL FISHING. This photograph, taken at the mill, shows a successful enterprise of the village's early years. Here, men load shad to be used for fertilizer. In 1921, Otto Wagner caught a 156-pound sturgeon in Lake Ontario. The fish contained 30 pounds of caviar, which sold at $3 a pound! (Courtesy of the Porter Museum.)

WARTIME. The terrorist attacks of September 11, 2001, have changed our waterfront by increasing the presence of border patrol and Coast Guard vessels. During World War II, boats were required to use large identification numbers for recognition by the Coast Guard. (Courtesy of the Porter Museum.)

PIERCE MARINA. Libby Pierce, an early organizer of the yacht club, stands in front of the marina south of the club. His early ancestor to the area was Eli P. Pierce. (Courtesy of the Porter Museum.)

WAITING FOR SPRING. Townspeople in the spring of 1980 are eager for the snow to melt, sailboats to color the waters during the Level Regatta, fisherman to launch at the fort dock, and the youth to embark on junior sailing lessons. (Courtesy of the Niagara Falls Public Library, Niagara Falls, New York.)

Two

COMMERCE AT
THE CROSSROADS

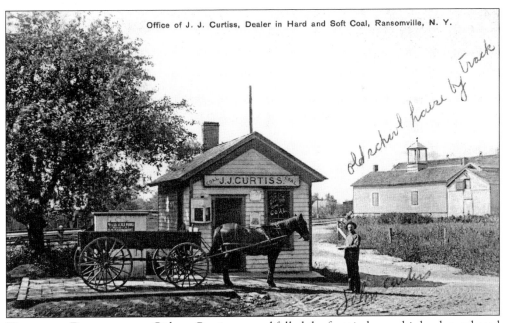

HAMLET OF RANSOMVILLE. Gideon Curtiss cut and felled the first timber on his land, purchased from the Holland Land Company in 1817. He was followed by his brother, Capt. Gilbert Curtiss, who came with his promised wife in a one-horse covered wagon. He cut a road when arriving at the Ridge in order to continue to Ransomville. (Courtesy of Lawrence Grimm.)

ICE-CREAM CONES. Ice cream continues to delight children young and old, and in 1916, an ice-cream factory was started by Charles Grambo. This company was in business for only about five years and was then abandoned. The building was sold to the American Legion. (Courtesy of the Ransomville Museum.)

THE RAILROAD DEPOT. Inside the depot, Fred Slocum (left) and Ellis Lisman wait for the train to bring mail and supplies into the hamlet. The train also transported townspeople to visit their neighbors in Elberta, shipped farm produce, and took students to the Falls for high school. (Courtesy of the Ransomville Museum.)

EVERYTHING YOUR HORSE NEEDS. The harness shop became Burmaster's Store, the building in which John, Don, and Clyde Burmaster were born. The store was located on the east side of Ransomville Road, across the street from the present Rite Aid. It was torn down in the 1960s. (Courtesy of the Ransomville Museum.)

NOTIONS AND THINGS. Robert Molyneux's general merchandise store opened in 1904. Sales on the first day he opened were $4.11. Numerous additions were made to the building in the early years. Today it is the site of the Ransomville Post Office. (Courtesy of the Porter Museum.)

SHAVE AND A HAIRCUT. Elton "Cockey" Tryon's barbershop was located west of the Bank Building. There was a poolroom in the rear. (Courtesy of the Ransomville Museum.)

BEAMS AND BOARDS. The original Fowler Sawmill was later converted to the Hubble Basket Factory, organized by G. Elgin Hubble in 1896. The building burned in 1941, leaving only the stone walls. The sawmill operated by George P. Moore was located east of Four Corners on the north side of Route 93. (Courtesy of the Ransomville Museum.)

THE NAMESAKE. The hamlet of Ransomville took its name from the Jehial Clark Ransom family. Although Gideon Curtiss arrived on the scene first, the meeting to decide the hamlet's name was attended by more Ransom than Curtiss family members. Here, in 1905, Bert Carter stands on the wagon along with, from left to right, Seymour Ransom, Frank Ransom, Kittie Clapsaddle, and W. H. H. Ransom Jr. (Courtesy of the Ransomville Museum.)

MERCANTILE BUSINESS. W. H. H. Ransom arrived in town in 1839. Continuing his uncle's mercantile business, he constructed the three-story brick building at the main crossroads to serve as a general store. Ransom also acted as a purchasing agent for apples, wheat, other grains, and wool. His mercantile included fur trade with Native Americans. Ransom owned 1,000 acres of land. (Courtesy of the Niagara Falls Public Library, Niagara Falls, New York.)

THE MASONIC TEMPLE. This imposing three-story building was completed in 1907. In early years, it housed the post office and State Bank of Ransomville. The second floor had a hall for entertainment and dances, and the top floor was the lodge room for the Masons. The Rochester Trade Association gathered here in 1914. (Courtesy of Lawrence Grimm.)

THE FUNERAL PARLOR. In the late 1890s, William Gentle founded a Main Street hardware store. His son Harry E. Gentle continued the hardware business and founded a funeral parlor in the converted blacksmith shop east of the store. Dayton Hardison, the first in Niagara County to have an undertaker's diploma and license, opened Hardison Funeral Homes in 1922. (Courtesy of Lawrence Grimm.)

FOUR CORNERS. The main intersection at Ransomville Road and Route 93 has changed little over the recent decades and remains the main traffic area for the community. First Niagara Bank has replaced Marine, with some building renovations. A gift shop now occupies the Corner Store, Porter Country Mart is on the southwest, and a beauty parlor and insurance office on the east. (Courtesy of the Niagara Falls Public Library, Niagara Falls, New York.)

VILLAGE OF YOUNGSTOWN. On the west side of Porter lies the village of Youngstown, whose settlement was neighbor to the fort. In this 1920s southward view of Main Street, trolley car tracks have replaced the stagecoach line. Route 93 is on the left side of the photograph, and the entrance to Water Street is between the Eldorado and Haskell's building. (Courtesy of the Niagara Falls Public Library, Niagara Falls, New York.)

THE EAST SIDE. The wagon and blacksmith shops are gone now. This postcard from the Youngstown Volunteer Fire Company's Labor Day parade in 1938 displays the shops on the east side of Main Street. Out of view on the right is the Meland Hotel, which in the 1950s was converted to an apartment house and barbershop. (Courtesy of the Porter Museum.)

THE WEST SIDE. The 1952 parade showcases the attractive brick opera house on the west side of Main Street. At the right edge of the photograph is the frame dwelling serving as the original village hall with a jail in the rear. Today, it is a parking area. (Courtesy of the Porter Museum.)

SUMMER AND WINTER OF 1921. Another of Main Street's brick structures, this building was constructed by B. D. Davis in 1854–1855. It was a general store operated by the Davis and Haskell families until well into the 20th century. The building was modernized by Kirk Hastings in the early 1970s and today includes apartments and a barbershop. (Above courtesy of Patricia Hutchinson Phillips; below courtesy of the Porter Museum.)

FLOUR AND WATER. The Stone Steam Flouring Mill on Water Street was erected in 1840 by Hezekiah H. Smith. In the business's early days, more than 200 barrels of grain were ground in a day. A storm later damaged the upper part of the building, and condominiums replaced the top floors of the mill. Today the first floor is a marine shop. (Courtesy of the Old Fort Niagara Association Inc.)

THE BARTON HOUSE. Alexander Barton constructed an early village tavern known as the Barton House about 1840. He sold it in 1893 to William J. Comerford, whose descendants owned the building until the 1990s. Rick Lohr recently restored the structure to its early style. The rear of the building views historic Fort George across the river in Canada. (Courtesy of the Porter Museum.)

"STRICTLY FIRST CLASS." The Eldorado Hotel, located on the northwest corner of Main and Water Streets, was built by F. C. Steele in the 1890s. Steele advertised the Eldorado as follows: "All modern improvements. Steam heat, gas and sanitary plumbing; good livery and barn attached. Just the place to spend the summer." The building was demolished in 1939. (Courtesy of the Porter Museum.)

THE FIREHOUSE. The Haskell Brothers sold farm machinery here in 1914. For a short period of time around World War II, the federal government owned the building and used it for a USO hall. It became the firehouse after the war. Located on Second Street across from the Catholic church, the building was demolished and replaced by the Marine Midland Bank, now HSBC Bank. (Courtesy of the Porter Museum.)

THE ONTARIO HOUSE. In 1842, Alexander Lane built the Ontario House on the site of the old Hathaway Tavern, which had burned during the War of 1812. Robert Guernsett and his wife were also early tavern keepers. The Ontario House was occasionally a gathering place for people known as the honest "Horse Thieves." The group, formed in the 1880s, aimed to protect citizens and search for stolen horses. Some of the members identified in a *Niagara Falls Gazette* article were Rennie Foster, Ray C. Tower, "Butch" Connors, Al Phillips, W. E. Eaton, Mr. Perrigo, Fred Pollow, Elbert Baker, Elmer Manning, Fred Dietz Jr., Charles Ayer, Martin Primus, Albert Robertson, and Mr. Foster. (Courtesy of the Porter Museum.)

Three

FORT NIAGARA

ENTRANCE TO THE FORT. Soldiers no longer stand at post at the south entrance. Today, a ticket stand greets tourists, townspeople, fisherman, and soccer players who treasure the fort, dock, beach, and park. (Courtesy of the Old Fort Niagara Association Inc.)

THE FRENCH CASTLE. In 1725, the Senecas gave their consent for the building of the stone house known as the "Castle." It became one of the most important fur-trading posts and strategic military positions, as it controlled the route to the other Great Lakes and the West. The legend of the Haunted Well inside the Castle delights children and adults alike. (Courtesy of the Old Fort Niagara Association Inc.)

DOC AND THE HOSPITAL. The hospital is located off the northeast corner of the parade group in this *c.* 1895 image. The driver of the buggy by the building is Dr. William J. Falkner. Colonel Raymond, post doctor, is seated to the right. In uniform on the steps is hospital steward Seibert, also an organist at St. John's Episcopal Church. (Courtesy of the Old Fort Niagara Association Inc.)

Light House Fort Niagara, N. Y.

THE GUIDING LIGHT. The first light on the Great Lakes was from the lantern room on the roof of the French Castle. The first whale oil–fueled lantern evolved to this lighthouse, erected outside the fort's walls in 1871. In 1900, a watch room was added. (Courtesy of the Porter Museum.)

THE 42ND REGIMENT. The Regiment of Infantry U.S. Volunteers, Company H, depart Fort Niagara for service in the Philippine Islands on October 30, 1899. Their service is marked at the fort by a monument located about 100 yards north of the officers club. (Courtesy of the Old Fort Niagara Association Inc.)

THE PARADE GROUNDS. Army mules form on the parade ground as the officers gather for morning exercises about 1917. Married officers' housing and the Niagara River are visible in the far left background. (Courtesy of the Old Fort Niagara Association Inc.)

A DEDICATED MULE. In the mid-1930s, orders were issued to put down all but the youngest and strongest army horses and mules. The mule Whiskey was a regimental favorite and had been in every engagement since the regiment's inception in 1901. After an appeal to the top brass, he was given special dispensation and lived out his days at the fort. (Courtesy of the Old Fort Niagara Association Inc.)

"ALWAYS AN ALLY." In 1935, Japanese admiral Isamu Takeshita toasts Col. Charles H. Morrow, decorated by Japan for his command in Siberia during World War I, at the officers club. Takeshita was quoted stating that Japan and the United States would never go to war against each other. This original officers club burned in 1936. (Courtesy of the Old Fort Niagara Association Inc.)

NEW RADIO EQUIPMENT. An ultramodern frequency radiotelephone transmitter and receiver are tested in 1938 by Pvt. Ronald Upchurch (left), Pvt. Kenneth C. Sanger (center), and Lt. Col. Frank E. Bonney. The new radio set was issued to the Communication Platoon Headquarters Company, 28th Infantry. (Courtesy of the Old Fort Niagara Association Inc.)

THE COMMISSARY. Prior to World War I, the commissary featured Bull Durham chewing tobacco and other items that helped make military life a little more comfortable. Postcards were available to send to family, friends, and sweethearts. (Courtesy of the Old Fort Niagara Association Inc.)

JESUIT CHAPEL. The Jesuit chapel located inside the French Castle was restored prior to this 1934 photograph. It is one of the oldest Catholic chapels in the country. (Courtesy of the Old Fort Niagara Association Inc.)

SOLDIERS AND MARKSMANSHIP.
Fort Niagara was renowned for
its soldiers' marksmanship and its
excellent 1,000-yard rifle range.
Although the soldier here, in
April 1941, is training on a 1903
model Springfield bolt-action
rifle, soldiers were issued the
M-1 Garand rifle, an eight-shot
semiautomatic introduced about
1937. (Courtesy of the Old Fort
Niagara Association Inc.)

AN AERIAL VIEW. This view, looking south over the fort in the 1940s, includes the auxiliary
hospital buildings and wards (four long white buildings). Just beyond them is the fort's fire
company, and at the upper edge of the photograph is the soldiers' barracks. (Courtesy of the Old
Fort Niagara Association Inc.)

SECRETARY OF WAR. On September 4, 1934, Secretary of War George H. Dern reviews the soldiers of the 28th Regiment on parade as part of the Four Nations Celebration and the dedication ceremonies for the restored Old Fort Niagara. (Courtesy of the Old Fort Niagara Association Inc.)

THE LaSALLE MONUMENT. This memorial was erected in 1934 and dedicated to Rene-Robert Cavelier Sieur de la Salle. The inscription reads, "LaSalle raised the first rude palisades of a Fort and from this base began his far voyaging in exploration of mid-America, the Ohio, the Great Lakes and the Mississippi to the Gulf of Mexico. . . . Through his courage, suffering and endurance came Christianity and civilization." (Courtesy of the Old Fort Niagara Association Inc.)

LIEUTENANT GOVERNOR. Malcolm Wilson, who served as lieutenant governor for almost four terms, from 1959 to 1973, under Gov. Nelson Rockefeller and as governor himself from 1973 to 1975, speaks with Chief Elton Greene (center) and an unidentified chief at a celebration. Wilson was endeared to the fort because of his own service as a summer guide. (Courtesy of the Old Fort Niagara Association Inc.)

THE COLD WAR. In 1959, Fort Niagara took on a new mission as the command center for a regional system of Nike guided ground-to-air missiles located in Cambria. Pictured here are Col. Michael J. Krisman (left), commander of the 2nd Artillery Group (air defense) and Fort Niagara, Captain Micinowski (center) of Battery B, and Colonel Woods of the 1st Missile Battalion. (Courtesy of the Old Fort Niagara Association Inc.)

THE LAST RETREAT. Soldiers gather for the last time on June 30, 1963, on the parade ground. With the retirement of the colors and conclusion of the day's retreat ceremonies, Fort Niagara ceased to exist as an active army base. This concluded more than 236 years as a military installation. (Courtesy of the Old Fort Niagara Association Inc.)

Four

PECKS AND THRESHING

BEFORE COMBINES. Elwin L. Harwick and his family prepare to thresh the grain in 1878. Wheat and other grains were cut by hand with a scythe and then shocked into bundles for threshing at the barn. The Harwicks lived on the south side of Route 93, west of Four Corners. Elwin was married to Ella Wille. (Courtesy of Lawrence Grimm.)

PACKING PEACHES. Peter Tower and his family pack fruit at the scale house at his Tower's Corners farm. An early settler, Peter reportedly helped construct a hopper for the Porter gristmill in Niagara Falls and assisted in the building of the first Goat Island Bridge. His direct ancestor came to America in 1637 from Hingham, England. (Courtesy of the Porter Museum.)

CONCORD GRAPES. Henry Dedrick Burmaster, born in 1837 in Hanover, Germany, established a farm on Ransomville Road north of Braley. The concord grapes in this *c.* 1904 photograph are said to be from the original vine on the Odd Fellows property in Lockport and are believed to be the first grapes introduced to Niagara County. Burmaster's granddaughter Doris stands with him. (Courtesy of Clyde Burmaster.)

RANSOMVILLE BASKET FACTORY. On May 31, 1895, the *Youngstown News* reported the basket factory would start on Monday mornings with an order for 50,000 peach baskets and smaller orders for berry, cherry, and plum baskets. The workers in this 1908 photograph include, from left to right, the following: (first row) Charles Estes and George Perry; (second row) Everett Goodfellow, Grace Bagley, Anna Wolfe, Gladys Ingraham, Mary Shaw, Henry Wolfe, Bryant Bagley, William Wolfe, and William Powley; (third row) Ernest Hillman, Gertrude Wolfe, Anna Clement, Allie Fowler, and Alice Stacey; (fourth row) Charles Grambo, Charles McColuf, Joseph Joblenski, Almeda Murray, M. McColuf, Edna Furman, Floyd Holmes, and William Allen; (fifth row) Ella Burmaster, Julie Schulze, Maria Neuman, Anna Lilm, William Neuman, and Fred Shirley. (Courtesy of the Ransomville Museum.)

SWIGERT'S EVAPORATOR. Brothers John and Henry Swigert built the evaporator west of Four Corners, on the south side of Route 93. Shortly thereafter, Henry bought out his brother and began a successful apple-drying operation. A cooperage was added in 1905. Swigert's Hall, located behind the Freys' home, is the only building remaining today. (Courtesy of the Ransomville Museum.)

APPLES FOR PROCESSING. Piles of apples await processing behind Swigert's, which was reportedly one of the largest apple-drying businesses in the world at the time. Russia even sent a delegation to study the agricultural methods used there. (Courtesy of the Ransomville Museum.)

THRESHING CREWS. Groups traveled from farm to farm to thresh grain. Farm wives were expected to feed these crews. George Cebern Truesdale, born in 1890, started threshing when he was just 16 years old and at one time had 164 different farmers lined up, waiting for him to cut their grain. (Courtesy of Lawrence Grimm.)

WINTER FRUIT TRIMMING. Fruit farmers trim during the winter when the trees are dormant. In 1940, this Baldwin apple tree required an extensive amount of time and effort. Today, farmers use root stocks designed to keep the size of the tree smaller.

NIAGARA POULTRY FARM. W. R. Curtiss started a poultry farm in 1887. Erected earlier, the Excelsior elevators were 30 by 60 feet in size with 24-foot posts and a storage capacity of 25,000 bushels. Wheat, barley, and other grains were threshed by farmers and brought to the elevators, where Curtiss shipped them out by rail. The rail car is visible in the above postcard depicting the poultry farm operation. Below, women pluck the feathers from the scalded chickens. (Both courtesy of the Ransomville Museum.)

AGRICULTURAL LEADER. The Curtiss Poultry Farm was considered the largest of its kind in the country. W. Roy Curtiss, along with his brothers Jay and Leo, pioneered in marketing to the Thousand Islands, Adirondacks, and New York City areas. In fact, the farm attracted worldwide attention for its agricultural practices including incubation. Russia, Japan, and other countries sent delegates to study the Curtiss methods. Thousands of ducks were hatched, raised, and sold. Continuing the family legacy, in 1953, Rex Curtiss raised 2,000 turkeys, kept a large number of laying hens, and operated a feed and milling business. (Courtesy of the Ransomville Museum.)

SAM AND DICK. David Courtland Baker's team of horses was an important part of his early farming operation. Baker was a poultry man raising from 1,600 to 1,800 layers. Much of his open land was devoted to grain crops for chicken feed and to hog raising. At this time, Niagara County was one of the state's ranking counties in hog production. (Courtesy of Audrey Baker Tower.)

APPLES ON CHURCH STREET. Farmers line up on Third Street, bringing their fruit to storage in bushel baskets. Youngstown Cold Storage is now closed, but Ransomville Storage, in operation since 1916, stores local fruit. A number of farmers also have some cold storage on their farms. (Courtesy of Youngstown Cold Storage.)

YOUNGSTOWN COLD STORAGE. In 1914, president L. S. Silberberg, treasurer G. H. Cothran, and secretary Howard A. Hopkins were noted on the stationery of the Western Niagara Fruit Growers Cold Storage Company. The business advertised 2,900 acres of peaches, 1,870 acres of apples, 582 acres of pears, 86 acres of quinces, 82 acres of plums, and 66 acres of cherries. It also claimed to be known all over the civilized world for flavor and quality. Above, the engine waits on the southeast side of the storage to transport fruit from the local farms. The rail line ran parallel to River Road south from Youngstown. Below is a northwest view of the building and its covered loading dock. Later, a dock was added on the southeast corner for tracks. (Both courtesy of Youngstown Cold Storage.)

FARM BUREAU COMMITTEEMAN. Here, Wilbur H. Shumaker sprays his fruit orchards with an unidentified tractor driver. Shumaker, serving as a committeeman for the farm bureau since its inception in 1912, was a vigorous proponent of scientific farming and a state leader in the movement for the packing of first-quality fruit. (Courtesy of the Porter Museum.)

CHECKING THE MELON CROP. Jim Allen checks melons on his Lake Road farm about 1950. In addition to fruit production, farmers grew field crops including a variety of vegetables, field and sweet corn, wheat, and cabbage. Today, there are significant acreage plantings of winter wheat, field corn, and cabbage in the town. (Courtesy of Betty Allen.)

A ROADSIDE STAND. A variety of produce is displayed roadside in the 1940s. Today, farmers continue to operate stands throughout the town in addition to selling at the Clinton-Bailey, Niagara Falls, and Tonawanda markets. (Courtesy of Betty Allen.)

BLESSING THE HARVEST. A cornucopia of fall crops and canned goods waits for a blessing in St. John's Episcopal Church in the village of Youngstown. (Courtesy of St. John's Episcopal Church.)

ON THE FARM. Children (above left) enjoy a summer's day on the Helms farm about 1927. Farmer Lawrence Baker (above right) looks over his corn crop. Glenn Sanger (below) stands by one of his father's calves in 1940 on their farm at Porter-Center and Route 93. Today, the Sangers have a farm market and bakery full of fruit pies, jams, and other pastries. (Above right courtesy of Phyllis Baker Hastings; below courtesy of Sandra Sanger Tuck.)

AGRIBUSINESS. These men are discussing the agriculture prices listed on the blackboard behind them. At the microphone is Al Fox, radio newsman of WHLD. The others are, from left to right, Dick Courter, Milford Parker, and two unidentified men. Milford and his father, Elton Parker, farmed over 300 acres, including 35 acres of fruit and a herd of 42 milking cows. (Courtesy of the Parker family.)

PASSING ON THE FARMING HERITAGE. "I want to be a farmer!" In 1951 as today, children remember their first tractor ride with their father and wait for the moment when they can sit on the tractor seat alone.

THE FAMILY FARM. Seagulls relish the freshly churned dirt in the spring of 2005 while the Pete and Jeff Baker family farming enterprise discs and cultipacks the field of Cleland Truesdale. The field is located on Lutts Road, adjacent to the Dietz farm and east of Tower's sweet cherry orchards. This is a sight that the community hopes will endure.

Five

READING, WRITING, AND ARITHMETIC

WAITING FOR SCHOLARS. Marion Williams Connor awaits her students at Rural School No. 10, on Balmer and Porter-Center Roads, one of 12 rural schools. In 1831, at a meeting of District No. 3 at Blairville and Creek Roads, David Canfield called a meeting where it was resolved that $3 be raised for the repairs of the hearth, a lock, and five panes of glass. (Courtesy of the Ransomville Museum.)

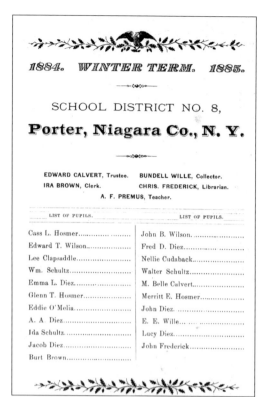

BROWN'S RURAL SCHOOL NO. 8. Located on the north side of Youngstown-Wilson Road, near Braley, was Rural School No. 8. On March 26, 1894, Friedrich Diez, the school's sole trustee, authorized collector John Wilson to pay Willie Schultz $4.25 for building fires and $5.50 to John McCormick for wood.

SCHOOL NO. 1. Around 1840, this brick schoolhouse on Main and Water Streets replaced the little one-story frame schoolhouse of 1819. It was also used for religious services held in the village until the First Presbyterian Church was built. (Courtesy of the Porter Museum.)

SCHOOL IN THE HAMLET. The earliest known school was a log cabin on McCracken's farm on Ransomville Road. Here, Ransomville classmates pose by the Baptist church. Ella Woolson is seated in front, and William Wisner, the commissioner, is on the right. (Courtesy of Lawrence Grimm.)

DISTRICT NO. 4. Teacher Isadore Cowan, standing in the back, poses with her students at Zittle's Corners in 1901. Pictured here, from left to right, are the following: (first row) Criss Sanger, Leon Sanger, Barbara Shippy, Harold Whittaker, Ray Whittaker, and Jennie Whittaker; (second row) Julia Clapsaddle, Anna Kneepel, and Rudolph Hillman; (third row) Jesse Martin, Webb Cowan, Belle Whittaker, and Trix Olmstead. (Courtesy of the Porter Museum.)

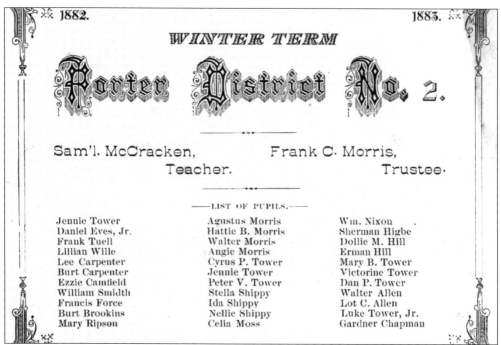

DISTRICT NO. 2. Located at Tower's Corners (the intersection of Route 93 and Creek Road), School No. 2 survives today as the residence of one of Peter Tower's many descendants, Mary Ann Tower Rolland, and her husband, Bill. (Courtesy of the Porter Museum.)

THE RED BRICK SCHOOL. This building has weathered the patter of many young feet. The main part was erected in 1892 at a cost of $8,000 and contained four rooms. Additions were constructed in 1919 and 1929. The first graduate with a Regents diploma in 1907 from Youngstown High School was Geraldine Hall. (Courtesy of the Porter Museum.)

CLASS OF 1890. Seen here, from left to right, are the following: (first row) Ina Dixon and David Smithson; (second row) Laura Olmstead, Louise Cowan, Lynn Martin, Trix Olmstead, teacher Donna Clapsaddle, Katie Clapsadde, Dora Olmstead, and Cora Olmstead; (third row) Belle Cowan, Blanche Clapsaddle, Alice Beach, Arthur Johnson, Guy Smithson, Wilfred Whittaker, Wallace Cowan, and Frank Martin; (fourth row) Bob Ripson, Dora Cowan, Bessie Cowan, Ernest Patterson, Lewis Olmstead, Merton Whittaker, and unidentified; (fifth row) Mabel Cornell, Ina Whittaker, Frank Johnson, Elton Cornell, Arthur Dixon, Nellie Johnson, and Elliott Whittaker; (sixth row) Ada Olmstead, Anna Harrington, Wilbur Cornell, Nellie Cornell, Gertrude Johnson, and Robin Cornell; (seventh row) Minister Bell and Sara Jeffords. (Courtesy of the Porter Museum.)

THE RANSOMVILLE SCHOOL. This school housing grades three through eight was used from 1900 to 1939 and was located at the site of the present Ransomville Fire Company. Primary classes were taught in an adjacent building. In 1907, Alex Gow was trustee; Jefferson T. Warren, collector; Arthur Curtiss, clerk; and William Wisner, commissioner. (Courtesy of Lawrence Grimm.)

CARRIE CARTER'S CLASS. Shown c. 1913 at the Porter Center School are, from left to right, the following: (first row) Arthur Baker, John Ripson, Russell Diez, and Harry Ripson; (second row) Fred Lloyd, Milton Perry, Lawrence Baker, Louis Diez, Courtland Baker, Dalton Diez, and Benny James; (third row) Florence Dean Clare, Myrtle James McLennan, May James Nichols, Herberta Shippy Chestnut, Mrs. Bell, and Elberta Baker Stacey; (fourth row) Gilda Perry, Carrie Carter, Winifred Diez Truesdell, Laura Zilm Myers, Eleanor Perry, and Florence James Smithson. (Courtesy of the Porter Museum.)

MISS SUNBALL'S CLASS IN 1938. Standing on the school steps in Ransomville are, from left to right, the following: (first row) Matthew Jerla, Phillip Clement, Neil Truesdell, Nancy Curtiss, Delores Magill, Clifford Collins, and Betty Myers; (second row) Jean Ricker, Jack Carew, Paul Markell, Virginia Ames, Eugene Ingraham, and John Burlingame; (third row) Joyce Colliver, Norma Barkow, Marjorie Rutherford, Stephen Handy, and William Stacey; (fourth row) Lois Drinkwalter, Elizabeth Fields, Neil Arnold, Casimera Jerla, Ruth Biehl, and George Perry; (fifth row) Suzanne Curtiss, teacher Elene Sunball, Jean Newman, and Marjorie Molyneaux. (Courtesy of the Ransomville Museum.)

YOUNGSTOWN SCHOOL, 1915 AND 1935. Shown above is the class of 1915. From left to right are the following: (first row) Theodore Adams, Park Taylor, Glenn Wagner, and Clarence Balcom; (second row) Mary Ann Walsh (teacher and principal), Evelyn Taylor, Mary Doty, Frances Stephenson, Ruth Clark, Catherine Murphy, Marion Hall, Nellie Robinson, Muriel Cothran, Helen Wagner, Garnet Clark, Lela Clark, and May Warner; (third row) Harry Adams, Tracy Taylor, Edgar Gore, Leroy Adams, Albert Taylor, James Allen, Wallingford Moon, Fred Crozier, Elizabeth Tower, Marion Eaton, and Frances Oneita Wagner. Below, first-grade students line up adjacent to the school on Third Street, waiting for the 1933 Field Day celebration. (Both courtesy of the Porter Museum.)

THE LUTTS DISTRICT. Located just north of Balmer Road, the Lutts District was known as School No. 11. Teacher Veronica Connor, standing here behind her class, later became the superintendent of schools for the Grand Island School District. Pictured with her are, from left to right, the following: (first row) Ruth Chaffee, Ramona McCollum, Arthur Martin, Marjorie Martin, Erva Broker, ? Chaffee, Marjorie Carter, Muriel Carter, Calvin Broeker, and Leon McCollum; (second row) Edward Mussell, Betty Chaffee, Clarence Hann, Waive Woodland, Oral Chaffee, Dorothy Broeker, Albert Hann, and Cleland Truesdale. (Courtesy of the Porter Museum.)

The Yellow School Bus. Children walked; sometimes Bob Comerford picked students up in a surrey-top wagon and brought them to school. Later, Dave Parkhill ran the first bus, and in 1934, Schultz Bus Lines was established. Here, Virginia (left), Gene (center), and Jack Johnson are ready to board the bus. (Courtesy of Porter Museum.)

The Valedictorian. Winifred Rose, standing by her students' artwork, gave the valedictory speech at the third annual commencement exercises of the Youngstown High School on June 24, 1929. Rose was presented with her diploma by Wilbur Shumaker, president of the board of education. She later received her degree from the state normal school in Brockport on June 11, 1935. (Courtesy of the Porter Museum.)

W. H. STEVENSON ELEMENTARY. These third- and fourth-grade students at the W. H. Stevenson Elementary School are identified from front to back, starting with the left row: (first row) Randall Zahno, Bonnie Burmaster, Gail Bills, and Robert Schultz; (second row) Sandra Davis, Judy Martin, Carol Carnrike, Carolyn Hessinger, Marvin Truesdale, and Robert Myers; (third row) Jane Martin, Merton Wiepert, Joyce Hillman, ? Pollow, Sonya Chylock, and Gary Jeffrey; (fourth row) Kenneth Drinkwalter, Clarence Mattoon (by the window), Wayne Clements, and Bruce Whitt; (fifth row) teacher Ada Schulze, Ronald Johnston, David Stott, Blair Frey, Victor Betts, and Harold Warner. (Courtesy of the Ransomville Museum.)

NOUNS, VERBS, AND *PARLEZ-VOUS*. Ruth Truesdale, English teacher, married Norm Townsend. Harry Godfrey taught French at Youngstown School. An unidentified young man rests on his bicycle behind the teachers. (Courtesy of the Porter Museum.)

GRADE SCHOOL TEACHERS. The school program included this photograph of the teachers. Pictured here, from left to right, are the following: (first row) Mrs. James, Miss Britton, Mr. Whittaker, Mrs. Adams, and Miss Blossom; (second row) Miss Pagluso, Mrs. Gaskill, Mrs. Shuey, Mrs. Comerford, Mrs. Martin, and Miss Kelly. Mrs. Comerford became an elementary principal when the Lewiston-Porter School District was centralized on the Creek Road campus. Classes began there in 1952. (Courtesy of the Porter Museum.)

THE PRINCIPAL. Many of the townspeople remember Edith Ripson's strong administration of the Youngstown School. Here, she is standing on the left, next to mathematics teacher Mrs. G. Haskell. (Courtesy of the Porter Museum.)

HIGH SCHOOL FACULTY. These high school teachers are, from left to right, as follows: (first row) Mr. Neumann, Mrs. Ripson, and Mr. Stevens; (second row) Miss Burg, Mrs. Haskell, Miss Harding, Miss Magavero, and Miss Batt. (Courtesy of the Porter Museum.)

GRADUATION IN 1940. The 1940 Youngstown High School graduates are, from left to right, as follows: (first row) Norma Drinkwalter, Marjorie Brown, Eva Broker, Adaline Pawlowski, Norma Allen, Olga Holody, Pat Maloney, and Marge Rodenbaugh; (second row) Mary Schultz, Kenneth Diez, Roderick Tower, William Johnston, Freddy Nelson, Richard Jones, George Kathan, Milton Kulak, and Joyce Hardison. In earlier days, some students took the train and attended Niagara Falls High School. After bus service began, students on the east side of town attended Wilson High School.

Six

CALLED TO SERVE

FLAG DAY PARADE. Children from the town march through the streets of Ransomville during the Flag Day parade in 1936 to honor the military personnel who have sacrificed to protect and defend our country and town throughout history. (Courtesy of the Ransomville Museum.)

FORT NIAGARA CEMETERY. Amidst the smoke from the 1905 model field gunfire, the oldest cemetery stands to honor those who served. Ordnance Sgt. Lewis Leffman was buried in this cemetery in 1885. He was the first enlisted soldier in the country to receive a federal pension and, along with his wife, donated land for the present village Episcopal church. (Courtesy of the Old Fort Niagara Association Inc.)

THE AMERICAN REVOLUTION. Windsor Johnson, a soldier of the Revolution, died on November 16, 1853, at the age of 92 years, six months, and seven days and was buried in the Tower Cemetery. He arrived from Vermont in 1832 in a covered wagon with his wife, Rebecca Nichols. Their descendants' surnames include Balcolm, Shumaker, Clark, and Buckley. (Courtesy of the Porter Museum.)

SERGEANT MAJOR. A soldier of the 25th and 28th Infantries, Harold Hutchison served in World War I and was stationed at Fort Niagara before going overseas. His wife, V. Helen Jarnot, worked for the postal service for 31 years and was assistant postmaster in Youngstown. Their son Lt. Harold Hutchison of the U.S. Air Force became the first Youngstown boy killed in action during World War II. (Courtesy of Patricia Hutchison Phillips.)

WORLD WAR I MEMORIAL. The World War I Memorial in Ransomville's Curtiss Cemetery honors the sacrifice of veterans. The memorial is dedicated to those who died in action, especially those from Ransomville, including Albert Chestnut, Wilbur Crane, and O. Leo Curtiss. Adjacent to the flag on the left are John Thompson, Seymour Ransom, and Reverend Hinckley. On the right are Mrs. Chestnut, Mrs. Warren Curtiss, Will Harris, and other townspeople. (Courtesy of the Niagara Falls Public Library, Niagara Falls, New York.)

THE 8TH NEW YORK HEAVY ARTILLERY. General Grant considered Cold Harbor to be his worst military blunder. While serving with Company E, Pvt. Albert Dietz (also known as Johann Albrecht Diez) was hit by three mini-balls on June 3, 1864. He was transported to Emory Hospital in Washington, D.C., where he died on June 23, and was buried in Arlington Cemetery. Dietz's commander, Col. Peter Porter, was also killed.

STATE TROOPERS. State trooper Fred Homedieu is on duty in Ransomville during the early 1920s. Troopers boarded at the Travelers Home, located at 2516 Main Street in Ransomville, before their station was built. (Courtesy of Lawrence Grimm.)

BALLOON BATTALION. On October 23, 1918, Harold Norman Whittaker was in a balloon battalion stationed in Virginia. As a boy, Harold had walked from his Porter Center homestead, at the southeast intersection of Route 93, to Ransomville, changed from boots to shoes at Ransom's store, then rode the train to Wilson to attend high school. He was the son of Norman Harrison Whittaker and Kate Moag. (Courtesy of Don Whittaker.)

LIFESAVING STATION. The crews of the government lifesaving station battled for lives on Lake Ontario, especially during the winters to help those trapped on the ice. The station was constructed in 1893 for $5,000. Today, the Coast Guard serves to protect our border. (Courtesy of the Porter Museum.)

THE ULTIMATE SACRIFICE. Lewis "Duke" Canfield, the son of Frank J. and Jessie Hamblin Canfield, was killed in action in France on August 12, 1944. (Courtesy of Katherine Baker Collard.)

EUROPEAN THEATER. John V. Simon (right), with his buddy Gord in France in 1945, served from February 1943 to April 1946. He marched behind Patton and received an honorable discharge, having served with the 353rd Infantry Regiment. His brother Edward was a soldier in the Royal Canadian Artillery. The horrific sights of the Holocaust, Normandy, and the war followed John throughout his life.

D-Day. Medic Willard Ransom Harris served under Lt. Col. Teddy Roosevelt Jr., the assistant division commander, and was attached to the 12th Infantry Antitank Company. General Eisenhower greeted them at South Hampton, England, after they had spent almost a week crossing the Atlantic on the *Europa*, a prized German ship captured in World War I. The unit landed at Utah Beach on June 6, 1944. (Courtesy of Gary Harris.)

A Veteran. James Chestnut was the son of William and Evelyn Chestnut and the husband of Dora Bradley, the daughter of Frank and Theda Lafler Bradley. The Bradleys lived on Foster Road (now known as Dickersonville Road) and attended the Porter-Center Methodist Church until it closed. (Courtesy of the Ransomville Museum.)

WOMEN IN THE MILITARY. This U.S. Navy photograph portrays Porter historian Vee Housman, tradevman second class petty officer, in 1959 while riding home in a TV2 navy jet fighter-trainer with Lt. Virgilio Simoncelli. Vee operated the link trainer at the Oakland Naval Air Station in California, providing simulated flight for pilot trainees. (Courtesy of Vee Housman.)

TACTICAL FIGHTER SQUADRON. Capt. Nelson L. Beard stands on the far right in front of his jet at Seymour Johnson Air Base in Goldsboro, North Carolina. He began his first operational tour at Hahn Air Base, Germany, in 1973 with the 496th Tactical Fighter Squadron. He now lives with his family in the historic Isaac Swain House. (Courtesy of Margaret S. Beard.)

PARATROOPER. Edward C. Eagan was a paratrooper in the U.S. Army's 82nd Airborne Division from 1954 to 1957 while stationed in Germany. Ed's sons Dennis and John both served in the air force. His surviving spouse, Nan Skimmin Eagan, and most of their family still reside in Porter. (Courtesy of Nan Eagan.)

SEMPER FIDELIS. Stirred by his Niagara Community College history professor, who had served in World War II and Korea, Todd Kozey stepped out on a road less traveled. In 1997, his boots hit the dirt of Paris Island, South Carolina, where he underwent boot camp. Today, he works for the EDO Corporation, which provides communications systems for the Marine Corps's amphibious assault missions. (Courtesy of Ed Kozey.)

VETERANS OF THE AGES. On May 31, 2004, the Veterans of the Ages Memorial was dedicated to all the men and women from the town who had served their country since the Revolutionary War. More than 1,000 names are listed on the kiosk adjacent to the stone in Veterans' Park.

Seven

ROBERT'S RULES
OF ORDER

PORTER OFFICIALS IN 1961. Town officials, from left to right, Judge Bemis, Lawrence Baker, Dan Wilson, and Reta Hanson follow "Robert's Rules" when conducting their meetings. These leaders succeeded constable Thadeus McIntyre, supervisor Dexter P. Sprague, and clerk Elijah Hathaway, who had been chosen at the earliest recorded town meeting of April 11, 1815. (Courtesy of the Porter Museum.)

WOMEN'S CHRISTIAN TEMPERANCE UNION. Meeting at G. Elmer Manning's house in the early 1900s are members of the Women's Christian Temperance Union, an organization choosing total abstinence from alcohol. They would pray in church and then march to the saloons to ask the owners to close their establishments. Adahlia H. Baker was the first president of the local group, formed in 1884. (Courtesy of the Ransomville Museum.)

May 9. 1933
Annual Meeting.
The Sierra Circle met with Mrs Hope Angevine on this date.
Meeting called to order by the President.
Minutes of the last meeting read and approved.
Under the head of business it was moved by Mrs Sierra Ransom that we give the sum of five dollars to the Ransomville Library—the motion was seconded, and after considerable discussion was carried
Roll Call—Annual dues to which 9 members responded, the Mrs Harris McCracken Peterson, S. Ransom, H. S. Ransom, D. Sanger, Jay Sanger, Uline & Eames
We then proceeded to the election of officer with the following result
Pres. .... Mrs Uline
First Vice. .... " Angevine
Second Vice. .... " Rogers
Secy. .... " Harris
Cor Secy. .... " McCracken
Librarian. .... H. S Ransom
Critic. .... Pr. Jay Sanger

STUDY CLUBS. Named for Sierra Ransom, the Ransomville study group Sierra Circle was organized in 1903 and has continued for decades with regular discussions of women in the Bible. The Youngstown Study Club has been meeting since 1922 and researches a theme each year. (Courtesy of the Ransomville Museum.)

THE CHOWDER KETTLE. The famous chowder served at the Youngstown Volunteer Fire Company's Field Day has a history of popularity in the town. In this early-1940s Labor Day image, Grace Wright helps prepare the chowder, which continues to sell out each year. (Courtesy of the Porter Museum.)

YOUNGSTOWN FIRST-AIDERS. Porter residents continue to be served by dedicated members of the Youngstown Volunteer Fire Company in times of need. Seen by the ambulance in this 1953 photograph are, from left to right, the following: (first row) Libby Pierce, Carl Acome, James Murr, Joe Agnello, Don Tower, and Joe Coolan; (second row) Charles White, Eddie Jaycox, Louie Mies, Len Renauff, Jenny Owens, Ken Comerford, Phil Zasucha, and Fred Wilkesmore. (Courtesy of the Porter Museum.)

PROGRAM.

Old Maid's Matrimonial CLUB.

CHARACTERS.

President Maribah Lovejoy .... Miss Eliza Robinson
Secretary Amerilla Haywood .... Miss Donna Clapsattle
Treasurer Priscilla Hope .... Miss Carrie Bullock
Prof. De Loffre .... Mr. Ernest Robinson
Monsieur Lereaux .... Mr. Wilbur Shumaker
Monsieur Zola .... Mr. Bert Carter

MEMBERS.

Selina Baxter .... Miss Margaret Went
Serena Grimshaw .... Mrs. Wm. Clapsattle
Mahala Minkley .... Miss Jessie Swain
Sara Jane Springster .... Miss Josie Lacy
Evangeline Smith .... Miss Louise Balmer
Anxiety Dohearty .... Mrs. W. C. Eaton
Patience Perkins .... Miss Carrie Balmer
Faith Montague .... Mrs. James Calvert

OLD MAID'S MATRIMONIAL CLUB. This Old Maid's Club program was likely performed at Pickwick Hall, a gathering place for musical performances, recitation, and debates at the corner of Second and Hinman Streets in Youngstown. It is an apartment building today. (Courtesy of the Porter Museum.)

THE MASONS. The past grands of Fort Niagara Lodge No. 716 are gathered on August 5, 1941. From left to right are the following: (first row) H. R. Haskell, B. J. Moon, and W. L. Morris; (second row) A. J. Barnum, C. F. Kolloff, F. L. Lutts, J. L. Thompson, and T. O. Rice. The Masons continue to run a very active lodge in Ransomville. (Courtesy of the Porter Museum.)

Camp Moss. Established about 1928, Camp Moss was located on Lake Road west of the Hosmer Cemetery and was used by both the Boy and Girl Scouts for a number of years. In this July 1928 photograph, Boy Scouts learn the skills to survive in the outdoors. (Courtesy of the Ransomville Museum.)

The Slowpokes. Ed Ortiz returned from the Korean War in 1952 and, with a group of friends, kept the local police busy by speeding. In 1955, Ortiz spearheaded the creation of a quarter-mile track behind his garage. A $50 weekly purse was generated by passing helmets, and in 1956, a new Ransomville Speedway was built. (Courtesy of the Ransomville Museum.)

RANSOMVILLE FIELD DAYS. Above, crowds fill the streets of Ransomville at Field Day on August 8, 1925. The celebration, continuing annually until the 1960s, was held on the first Saturday in August. Below, townspeople enjoy the Ransomville Fire Company parade. The audience lines the south side of Main Street, Route 93, at Four Corners. Cliff Connor's garage appears on the left. The small white building in the center was a jail at that time. Today, the other building facing Ransomville Road is a beauty parlor. (Both courtesy of the Ransomville Museum.)

THE MOTHERS' CLUBS. Attending a gathering on January 9, 1962, are, from left to right, the following: (first row) Gertrude Kroatz and Nell Truesdell; (second row) Donna Clark, Gusty Raer, Margaret Oliphant, Olive Hastings, Irene Shea, Inez Truesdell, and Ida Myers. A number of these groups existed, including the Elberta Mother's Club, Ransomville Mother's Club, and Modern Mother's Club. (Courtesy of the Ransomville Museum.)

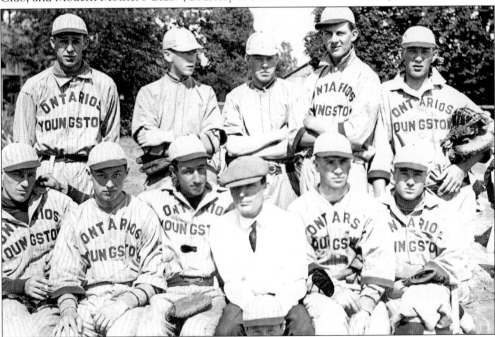

ONTARIOS BALL TEAM. The informal Mudhens played at Tower's Corners before organized teams like the Ontarios. Identified only by their surnames, the players are, from left to right, as follows: (first row) Kneeshaw, Carmick, Taylor, manager Monahan, Murphy, and Hall; (second row) Gates, Hopkins, Howard, Whitney, and Cook. Haskell, the mascot, appears at the very bottom of the photograph. (Courtesy of the Porter Museum.)

RANSOMVILLE FIRE COMPANY. On January 1, 1924, a devastating fire broke out in the early morning hours. Smith's drugstore, Neumann's grocery store, Liebow's Barber Shop on the corner, the Navel and Northern Garage, and part of the Methodist parsonage were burned. The Ransomville Fire Company was formed with nine members and firefighting equipment of a hand-drawn cart and bucket brigade. Earl Dodge served as the first chief, handling the calls from his house. The first fire hall was a barn on the lot where the post office is today. The present hall was built in 1960. It has been the site of community benefits, celebrations, and the first highly successful cabbage festival in 2004. (Courtesy of the Ransomville Museum.)

Eight

HISTORIC TRUST IN GOD

CENTENNIAL PARADE OF 1976. St. John's Lutheran Church of Youngstown celebrates with the townspeople by decorating a float for the 1976 centennial parade, a witness to its faith in Christ. (Courtesy of the Porter Museum.)

RANSOMVILLE BAPTIST CHURCH. This church was organized on February 8, 1834, built on land purchased from Jehial Clark Ransom, and dedicated on May 20, 1841. The bell placed in the tower in 1852 also served as the community fire alarm until 1924. The church's front pillars and porch were added in 1926. (Courtesy of Lawrence Grimm.)

DEDICATION OF CHURCH ORGAN. The electric organ was installed at the Ransomville Baptist Church as a memorial to those who gave their lives during World War II. On July 14, 1946, there was a special dedication service. Tower chimes installed in 1952 can still be heard throughout the hamlet. (Courtesy of Sue N. Mirabelli.)

REVEREND FATHERS. Rev. W. E. Nixon (left) and Rev. A. C. French stand in front of St. John's Episcopal Church, on Main Street in Youngstown, on May 16, 1948. The first rector of the church was promised a yearly salary of $200, a horse to make his rounds, and 200 pounds of horse feed a month. (Courtesy of St. John's Episcopal Church.)

"AGNUS DEI." Above the entry in this 1957 photograph of St. John's Episcopal Church of Youngstown is the octagonal Lamb of God window. The style of the country church is Carpenter Gothic from a design by Richard Upjohn. The 600-pound bell, forged at Troy in 1884, was shipped on the Erie Canal to Lockport and then carried on a horse-drawn cart to Youngstown by Isaac Lloyd. (Courtesy of St. John's Episcopal Church.)

LAYING THE CORNERSTONE. In 1905, Reverend Wells presides over the laying of the cornerstone for the Methodist church on East Main Street in Ransomville. (Courtesy of Lawrence Grimm.)

HUNDREDTH BIRTHDAY. This postcard view of the Methodist Episcopal church was taken in 1919. Known today as the Ransomville United Methodist Church, the structure is 100 years old. (Courtesy of Lawrence Grimm.)

WESLEYAN METHODIST. On the corner of Academy and Ransomville Roads, the former Wesleyan Methodist Church has been converted to an apartment building. Farther south, at 3924 Ransomville Road, is a modern brick structure for the Ransomville Free Methodist congregation. (Courtesy of Lawrence Grimm.)

EARLY METHODISTS. In 1877, the Free Methodist Church was built at 3596 Lake Street, now Ransomville Road. No longer used as a church, this building now houses Ransomville Antiques. Another Methodist church, this one on Porter-Center Road, is a small manufacturing building today. Howard and Dorothy Canfield Baker were the first to be married in the Porter-Center church. (Courtesy of the Porter Museum.)

SENIOR MEMBERS. Walter Gratz and Howard Koepke were the seniors of St. John's Lutheran Church of Youngstown in 2001. Gratz, pictured on the left in the above image, helped roll the original church on logs from Creek Road to Third Street. As seen below, the original structure is a residence today. (Left courtesy of St. John's Lutheran Church.)

A RURAL CHURCH. Fillmore Chapel was first organized as a Methodist Episcopal class meeting about 1821 at the home of George Ash with 14 charter members. It was named for Rev. Gleason Fillmore, an early Methodist pioneer. The current church building was erected at the intersection of Youngstown-Wilson and Ransomville Roads in 1852. (Courtesy of the Porter Museum.)

A HOUSE OF PRAYER. The First Presbyterian Society of the Town of Porter was founded in 1823. Rev. Ebenezer Everett, a home missionary from the Presbytery of Rochester, is credited with being Youngstown's first Presbyterian minister. After his suggestion to organize a church here, a planning meeting was held at the residence of Ashbel G. Hinman. (Courtesy of the Porter Museum.)

FROM COOPERAGE TO CHURCH. Rev. Francois Dollier de Casson, a Sulpician priest, celebrated the first mass on the east side of town. Founded as a mission in 1830, St. Bernard's Catholic Church (above) was served by the Vincentian Fathers of the Seminary of Our Lady of the Angels. Beginning in 1846, the former cooperage, situated at the corner of Second and Hinman Streets in the village of Youngstown, was used as a church until it was razed in 1948. Below is an image of the church sanctuary. (Both courtesy of St. Bernard's Catholic Church.)

FORT NIAGARA CHAPEL. Rev. Joseph Kennedy was assigned parish priest of St. Bernard's Church in 1946. In 1948, the chapel was purchased from the War Assets Administration and moved from Fort Niagara under the direction of Rev. Andrew Pronobis. On the sides of the altar, on the left over the door, an inscription indicates Chaplain L. Nattress and on the right, Chaplain F. J. Ward. Under the direction of Msgr. J. Thomas Moran, wings have been added to the church structure, the altar and pews redesigned, and the old panes replaced with beautiful glass windows depicting the sacraments, saints, and the fort chaplain. (Courtesy of St. Bernard's Catholic Church.)

A Preacher. An unidentified pastor preaches in the sanctuary in the First Presbyterian Church of Youngstown. Many changes and additions have altered the physical structure of the church. The congregation continues to grow, and its ecumenical community blesses Porter by welcoming all townspeople for meetings, concerts, and programs. (Courtesy of the First Presbyterian Church.)

Nine

OUR FAMILY PHOTO ALBUM

N. D. HASKELL, M.D. The son of John Haskell and Margaret Reed, Nelson Haskell married Elvira E. Davis. In 1890, his name graced the impressive sign on the Haskell Building, located at the village's main crossroads, which at that time housed the post office and hardware store. (Courtesy of the Porter Museum.)

FIRST SETTLER. John Lloyd, a soldier of the fort's garrison in 1799, settled about three miles from the fort in 1801. The Bible of his daughter Marcelia Lloyd Ripson notes that he was one of the soldiers who attended, with military honors, the body of George Washington to the grave. John's grandson Isaac served in the 8th New York Heavy Artillery and was held in the notorious Confederate Libby Prison in Virginia. (Courtesy of the Porter Museum.)

WEDDING ANNIVERSARY. Elton Tarbell Ransom and his wife, Alice Harriet Taylor, celebrate their 25th anniversary on June 7, 1901, with family. Elton was the son of William Henry Harrison Ransom. (Courtesy of the Ransomville Museum.)

TIN PLATE PAINTED PORTRAIT. Henry H. Hand (right) and his wife, Maria Johnson Hand (below), purchased a farm in the town of Porter in 1857. Alonzo Brookins built their home at the northwest corner of Dickersonville and Youngstown-Lockport Road in 1864. This intersection was known as Moss's Corners and later as Hand's Corners. The house has always been occupied by Hand or his descendants, currently by James and Phila Ibaugh. Phila is the great-great-granddaughter of Henry and Maria. The original farmland is still owned by Hand's great-grandchildren—Glenn Sanger, Shirley Sanger Canfield, Jeanette Sanger Brooks, and Susan Sanger Schafer.

GERMAN IMMIGRANTS. Johann Friedrich Diez and his wife, Anna Barbara Holder, emigrated to the town in 1867 from Dettingen unter Teck with their infant son Jacob. They arrived after an arduous journey aboard the immigrant ship SS *Union*, which had left Bremen destined for New York City. Friedrich's brother John picked them up at the Lockport train depot with a sleigh during a winter storm. Friedrich owned five farms, the earliest being the land now known as Four Mile State Park. The east line of this farm is called Dietz Road. Pictured in this *c.* 1886 family photograph are, from left to right, the following: (first row) Friedrich, Bessie, Anna Barbara, Christina, and Mary; (second row) John and William; (third row) Fred Jr., Albert, Jake, and Lucy. The eldest daughter, Emma, does not appear. Many Diez descendants live in the town today. Diez was also known as "Dietz." (Courtesy of Patricia Lloyd.)

FROM JEFFERSON COUNTY. Samuel Shippy arrived in Porter in 1851. He married a local girl, Chloe Henry, built a home, and started a farm at the edge of the village of Youngstown. He worked as the town highway commissioner and as a well-respected carpenter and farmer. After his wife died, he married Henrietta Churchill. Samuel fathered 10 children. (Courtesy of Harold Shippy.)

THE IRISH. Timothy J. Murphy (center, with mustache), a first-generation American, stands by the Ontario House with unidentified family members. He and his wife owned this property from 1890 to 1913. Timothy married Hattie Bell Morris and had two children: Lewis and Grace. Early Catholic church records show a number of Irish families in the area, including the Murphys. (Courtesy of the Porter Museum.)

HARWICK FAMILY. Grandma Harwick (above left) sits in her rocker. This Harwick house (above right) was situated on the north side of Route 93 in Ransomville. The main house and barn were on the south side of the road. Ethel Harwick (left) stands in front of some family plants about 1895. The Harwick family lived next door to Carlos and Sarah Brookins, according to the 1880 census. (All courtesy of Lawrence Grimm.)

AN INVENTOR AND HIS FAMILY.
Carlos Brookins (right) was a farmer
and inventor, designing and patenting
an elevator safety device that was used
globally. He married Sarah Gunn. The
Brookins family dates back to 1638
Boston, where members owned the
Salutation Inn, the later site of secret
discussions and propaganda for the
American Revolution. Below, May
Brookins (left), Lola Inez Brookins
(center), and Florence enjoy a
summer's day in 1903. (Courtesy
of Lawrence Grimm.)

BROCK'S MONUMENT. On a 1913 visit to the memorial in Queenston, Ontario, are Mary Jane Schreiber Burmaster (left), Ida May Brookins Fredricks (center), and Hattie Barry Storrie. Mary was related to General Brock, a Canadian hero of the War of 1812. (Courtesy of Lawrence Grimm.)

OLD-TIME BROADWAY STAR. Bradley Davis Haskell starred on Broadway in the early 1900s, appearing in *Queen of the Highbinders*, *The Girl in the Taxi*, *The Seven Keys to Baldpate*, and *Officer 666*. With Frank Striker of future *Lone Ranger* fame, Haskell produced chillers for WEBR radio in Buffalo. Pictured here, from left to right, are brothers Harry, Bradley (sitting), C. Ray, and H. Roy Haskell. (Courtesy of the Porter Museum.)

FAMILY GATHERING. Seen in 1914 are, from left to right, the following: (sitting on the grass) Dedrich ?, Chester ?, Marie Korff, and Dorothy Schultz; (sitting) Irene Korff (holding Harold Korff), Theodore Schultz, Hannah Schultz, Edith Schultz, Clara Boidle Klamer (holding an unidentified baby), and Sarah Schultz Burmaster (holding Lorraine); (standing) Fred Andrews, Louis Boidle, Hattie Schultz, Theodore Schultz, Bill Korff, and John Burmaster. (Courtesy of the Ransomville Museum.)

LADIES' OUTING. Elizabeth Thompson, holding a purse on her lap, was the daughter of John Diez and Christina Wilson and the niece of Friedrich Diez. She was born in 1864 and died in Ransomville in 1938. Pictured are, from left to right, the following: (first row) Elizabeth Thompson, Estella Dutton, Myra Moss, and Edith Ayer; (second row) Mrs. Moss, Mrs. George Cothran, Mrs. John Buckley, and Martha Dutton. (Courtesy of the Porter Museum.)

SLEIGH RIDE. With enough snow to use the sleigh, Blair Frey returns home after a ride with his granddaughter in Ransomville. (Courtesy of the Ransomville Museum.)

FOSTER'S HARDWARE. Mary Brookins (left) and Ida Brandt Foster sit in the sun. Ida and her husband ran the hardware store in Ransomville where the present Stevenson's Hardware is located. (Courtesy of Lawrence Grimm.)

POLISH IMMIGRANT. Caroline Sciera came to the town of Porter with her parents, Karolina and Peter, after their 1909 emigration from Bochnia, Poland. Caroline, her husband, Martin Holody, and their family operated the Ontario House for more than 50 years. Martin and Caroline were described by their family as "young at heart and able to deal with change. . . . They taught us how to understand [and] deal with people, to accept people for who they were, and try and find the good and best in others." Their grandson Eddie Wojcik is the Ontario House's current proprietor. (Courtesy of Edward Wojcik.)

THE COUSINS. The children of Elbert and Emily Baker and his brother Arthur gather about 1920. Shown here, from left to right, are the following: (first row) Arthur, Frank, Mildred, and Howard; (second row) Elberta, Esther, Zilpha, Courtland, and Lawrence. Esther and Zilpha were the daughters of Arthur and Martha Baker. Their ancestor David Baker came to Porter from East Hampton; he was the eldest son of Daniel, a Revolutionary War soldier. (Courtesy of the Ransomville Museum.)

THEY TOWER AMONG MEN. Four generations of the descendants of early settler Peter Tower stand by the house at 1647 Youngstown-Wilson Road, owned today by Dan Tower. Standing, from left to right, are George P. Tower (also known as Porter Baldwin), born 1896, married to Adelaide Thomas; George Pearce Tower, born 1836, married to Elizabeth Peet; Porter Baldwin Tower, born 1869, married to Myrtie Tower; and Richard Pierce Tower, born 1920, married to Margaret Truesdale. At one time, their pioneer ancestor to the town, Peter Tower, provided coffins for nearly everyone in the area and produced some of Niagara County's famed fruit. Today, Tower descendants continue to grow fruit and plant crops on more than 1,000 acres in the town. (Courtesy of Tom Tower.)

AN OLD BOYFRIEND. Merton Truesdell, the son of Andrew D. Truesdell and Hattie L. Bonesteele, poses for a Niagara Falls postcard photograph in 1913. On the back of the card is written, "Old boy friend of Inez." (Courtesy of Lawrence Grimm.)

ENJOYING THE DAY. In the summer of 1950, Carl Falkner (left), Bernie Brown (center), and Walter "Gery" Henry smile for Mr. Gerguson, the lighthouse keeper at the fort, as he snaps the shutter. (Courtesy of the Porter Museum.)

A New Baby and Friends.
To the right, Veldren and James
Allen pose with with their new
baby, Jean, in 1921. Veldren
is the daughter of Herbert
Lee Shippy and Blanche
Clapsaddle. James Leroy Allen
is the son of Walter and Olive
Allen. Below, friends for life
Herb Allen and Bill Canfield
celebrate Herb's birthday about
1936. Pictured from left to right
are Milo Clark, unidentified,
Herb, Bill, two unidentified,
Guy Myers, Doug Andrews,
and Charlie Clark. (Both
courtesy of Betty Allen.)

DESCENDANTS OF RANSOMVILLE ABOLITIONISTS. Dorothy (left), Willard (center), and Walter Harris were the children of Dr. Willard Harmon Harris and Almira Jeffery. Dr. Harris, active in early temperance efforts, was considered a "forward-thinking man" and had attended veterinary school in Quelph. (Courtesy of Gary Harris.)

FROM ULSTER COUNTY. In 1935, Jack (left), Suzanne (center), and Philip Ransom Jr. stand in front of their home in Ransomville. Their ancestor Jehial Clark Ransom came to this area at the age of 23 on foot from Ulster County in 1826. (Courtesy of Lawrence Grimm.)

A "G-MAN." Henry Sunball Jr. (far left) worked on the Dillinger case. Henry Sunball III (center) has his arms around his father and grandfather in this image from the late 1930s. (Courtesy of Lawrence Grimm.)

DUTCHMAN'S PIPE. A 100-year-old Dutchman's pipe vine is the backdrop for this 1936 gathering of local boys. Seen here, from left to right, are the following: (first row) Francis Ross, Bev Ross, and Paul Marabell; (second row) Frank Markell, Duane Matthews, Lawrence Grimm, and Bert Ross. (Courtesy of Lawrence Grimm.)

EYES LIKE DIAMONDS. For more than five decades, the Holody sisters helped serve the patrons—and their families—at the Ontario House, known to townspeople as "the Stone Jug." Olga Holody Matthews (left), Eugenia Holody Wojcik (center), and Renata Holody Sikoski are pictured here. In the late 1930s and early 1940s, people made the rounds of the bars in the village, including Michael's and Ferguson's (now Brennan's Irish Pub), Comerford's, the Jug, the Old Fort Inn, Meland's, and the Rathskeller in the Eldorado, run by the Jeffords. The Holody sisters' father, Martin, cautioned his daughters, "The men [soldiers] will tell you your eyes are like diamonds, but remember they have a girl back home!" (Courtesy of Edward Wojcik.)

PIONEER PICNIC. During the late 1800s, families began to gather for what became known as the Pioneer Farmer's Picnics, celebrated at the park in Olcott. The early photograph of the Ransom family above depicts some of the early settlers in whose memory the gathering is held. Grace Seymour Ransom is on the porch, Phil is on the pony, Seymour Ransom stands, and Marjorie and Jack appear in the carriage. At the picnic in the *c.* 1934 image to the right are, from left to right, the following: (first row) Kenneth George Diez and Hazel Beatrice Diez; (second row) John Frederick Diez; his wife, Edna Winifred Jeddo; and John J. Diez.

FLAG DAY. Townspeople gather for a Flag Day celebration at Fort Niagara in the mid-1930s. Sara Swain, the granddaughter of early settler Isaac Swain, is identified as the woman with her head bowed. William Kincaid, on the far right, was a leader in the restoration at the fort. The flag that flew over the fort during the War of 1812 is considered to be one of the most significant in the history of our country. When the fort fell to the British, Sir Gordon Drummond presented the flag to the king of England, who was not interested in it. Drummond therefore kept it in a Scottish castle, where it remained until purchased by the fort. The flag is now being restored. (Courtesy of the Niagara Falls Public Library, Niagara Falls, New York.)

WEDDING BELLS. In the photograph to the right, taken on April 17, 1946, Lawrence Grimm of Ransomville smiles with his new bride, Verna Watson, a "city" girl from Model City. Below, from left to right, Walter Diez, Helen Henry Diez, Marion Henry, and Harold Mudge pose for Marion and Harold's wedding photograph. Helen was the maid of honor for her sister. (Both courtesy of Lawrence Grimm.)

HIPPOCRATIC OATH AND HOUSE CALLS. The town of Porter has known a number of doctors. A favorite, Dr. John Plain began his practice in 1904 and served the community for more than 50 years. Some of his predecessors and colleagues were Drs. Hyde, Catlin, Falkner, Skinner, Long, Bosserman, Gray, Cook, Smith, McBain, Bright, and Clark. The Ransomville Community Council advertised for a doctor about 1949. In response came Dr. Salvatore Piazza, seen discussing administrative policies with Miss Ianello in this image from a program about the Ransomville Hospital, established by "Doc" in 1952. It opened with 20 beds and today serves as a residential senior center. (Courtesy of the Ransomville Museum.)

OUR GRANDPARENTS. Many in Porter are fortunate to have lived near their grandparents, benefitting from their love and wisdom. In the above image, Grandma Emily sits with her grandchildren. From left to right are Phyllis Baker, Kay Baker, Emily Wolfe Baker (holding namesake Emily), Ann Baker, and Audrey Baker. In the front right, on the first steps, are Paul Baker and Jean Oderkirk. In the photograph below, Jim Allen gives grandchildren Bonnie (left), Mark (center), and Kenny a tractor ride. (Above courtesy of Katherine B. Collard; below courtesy of Betty Allen.)

ALL GROWN UP. In 1952, the Harris clan gathered for a photograph. From left to right are Walter, Varion, Janet Marion, Betty Jane, Ruth Lucille, Dorothy M., John Burdette, and Willard Ransom Harris. The Eldridge Harris home, built about 1850 on the east edge of the hamlet of Ransomville, provided refuge for runaway slaves as part of the Underground Railroad. Many in Ransomville held strong abolitionist views. Aunt Adelaide told Walter that the Curtiss home, across from Gates Lumber Yard, was also a station house for hiding slaves. (Courtesy of Gary Harris.)

PORTER'S HISTORICAL SOCIETY. Cora Gushee stands adjacent to one of the signs erected by the Porter Historical Society. Porter Town Hall is to the right of the sign. (Courtesy of the Porter Museum.)

A COUNTRY LAWYER. John Victor Simon performed house calls, counseled people on the streets, and walked clients to their cars. Simon argued successfully pro bono in a 1967 precedent-setting case that required school districts to provide textbooks for all students in nonpublic schools. As Niagara County attorney in 1975, he appeared before Chief Justice Burger and the U.S. Supreme Court, which he called his "proudest moment as an attorney," and with Robert Abrams, state attorney general, filed the Love Canal suit against Hooker Chemical. He made St. John's Law School history by being the first to marry a classmate, Salome Authier, who was working as a research clerk for John Foster Dulles, the senior partner at the firm of Sullivan and Cromwell. Pictured in this family photograph are, from left to right, the following: (first row) Vivian, Louise, and Yvonne; (second row) Suzanne, Emery, John (holding Jeanne), Salome, Marie, and Gerianne; (third row) Juliette, John Jr., Jacqueline, and Nannette. (Courtesy of Simonsons Photographers.)

HISTORIAN EXTRAORDINAIRE. Cora Frances Anderson married Gordon Clark Gushee in 1925 and became 102 years young on March 10, 2005. She was the town historian for more than three decades, retiring only a few years ago. The town is deeply grateful for her lifelong passion to study and preserve its past. (Courtesy of Phyllis Edwards.)

Ten

HOME SWEET HOME

ONE OF THE OLDEST. Peter Tower arrived in 1815, when the town was still a wilderness. He bought 100 acres of land and built a store at the intersection of Route 93 and Creek Road, known today as Tower's Corners. The house had a six-partitioned brick basement. Denny Greene later moved the house farther north and used some of the original bricks for fireplaces. (Courtesy of the Porter Museum.)

CARTER'S BRICK HOMES. Pioneer builder John Carter settled in Youngstown in 1848, established a brickyard, and built his home and barn, which would become a focal point of church activity for nearly a century. His boat was reportedly used numerous times to help runaway slaves cross the river to Canada. Carter built the retaining walls around the fort, the Pillars home on River Road, Hennepin Hall in Lewiston, the Haskell building on Main Street, and three houses on Porter-Center Road (for the Quades, Smithsons, and Bakers). Here, the Baker family stands in front of the homestead, located south of Zittle's Corners. (Courtesy of the Ransomville Museum.)

ARCHITECT AND CARPENTER. In 1864, Alonzo Brookins built this home at the northwest corner of Route 93 and Dickersonville Road for the Hands. Brookins's homes are distinguished by the circular frames at the top of the doors and windows. The halls of his homes generally include a winding staircase with beautifully turned spindles. The Caroline Ransom Burlingame House, at 3596 Lake Street, is another built by Brookins.

A STURDY COBB HOUSE. The unique construction of the Samuel Shippy house, built around 1860, involves lumber laid between the frame, board by board. Lumber was plentiful during that time period. The well-maintained Shippy orchards and home have been continually owned and operated by Samuel's descendants. Neal Shippy now farms his great-grandfather's land. (Courtesy of Harold Shippy.)

HOUSES OF COBBLESTONE. A few cobblestone houses stand in town. Some of these were built by masons previously employed to construct the Erie Canal. This home was built in 1836 on the foundation of the former Swain house, which was burned by the British during the War of 1812. On the night of December 18, 1813, the British marched up River Road during a winter storm. William Swain recalled that the army was so quiet moving past the house, the family did not hear anything. In fact, troops entered the fort without a shot being fired. (Courtesy of the Old Fort Niagara Association Inc.)

VILLA ST. VINCENT. This benevolent home was established in order to help destitute orphans and young girls. The children were cared for by the Daughters of Charity of St. Vincent de Paul, whose mother house is in Albany today. Edna Jeddo lost her mother when she was only two years old and spent time at the villa before marrying John Diez. After the buildings were razed in 1957, the villa chapel was moved across the street to become the St. John's Episcopal Church hall. Edna, who was endeared to the nuns, worshiped with her family at St. John's throughout her life. The south end of the orphan's home is visible in the photograph above. Below is a west view of the villa from Main Street. This is the present site of the Villa Condominiums. (Both courtesy of the Old Fort Niagara Association Inc.)

BIBLIOGRAPHY

Ames, Donald B. *People, Places and Happenings along the Niagara.*

Dunnigan, Brian Leigh. *A History and Guide to Old Fort Niagara.* Youngstown, New York: Old Fort Niagara Association Inc., 1900.

"Honest 'Horse Thieves' Met at Hotel in Youngstown to Help Fight Crime." *Niagara Falls Gazette.* August 14, 1954.

Housman, Vee. Porter 1 Genealogy Database. Porter Historical Museum.

Loker, Donald E. *Lewis Leffman.* Lockport, New York: Niagara County Historical Society, 1974.

Pool, William, ed. *Landmarks of Niagara County, New York.* Syracuse, New York: D. Mason and Company, 1897.

Reed, I. Richard. *Evolutionary History of Niagara County, New York.* Lockport, New York: Niagara County Historian's Office, 1978.

Williams, Edward T. *Niagara County, N.Y. 1821–1921.* Chicago, Illinois: J. H. Beers and Company, 1921.

"Youngstown, Also 100 Years Old, Began Career as Supply Station for Garrison at Old Ft. Niagara." *Niagara Falls Gazette.* May 17, 1954.